USING
MAKERSPACES
FOR SCHOOL PROJECTS™

10 GREAT MAKERSPACE PROJECTS USING

SCIENCE

ERIN STALEY

Rosen
YA™
New York

Published in 2018 by The Rosen Publishing Group, Inc.
29 East 21st Street, New York, NY 10010

Library of Congress Cataloging-in-Publication Data

Names: Staley, Erin, author.
Title: 10 great makerspace projects using science / Erin Staley.
Other titles: Ten great makerspace projects using science
Description: New York City : Rosen Publishing, 2018. | Series: Using makerspaces for school projects | Includes bibliographical references and index. | Audience: Grade 6–12.
Identifiers: LCCN 2016056493 | ISBN 9781499438482 (library bound)
Subjects: LCSH: Makerspaces—Juvenile literature. | Science—Study and teaching—Activity programs—Juvenile literature.
Classification: LCC TS171.57 .S73 2018 | DDC 507.8—dc23
LC record available at https://lccn.loc.gov/2016056493

Manufactured in the United States of America

CONTENTS

INTROD

Some science projects focus on engineering while others are experimental and involve experiments.

S cience is everywhere—in the sports you play, the rainbow outside your window, and the mobile device you use to stay connected to the world at large. Science studies the world around us, asking who, what, when, where, why, and how. It explores function and reaction—all in an effort to better understand why things work the way they do, and to solve pressing problems.

Science has two branches: life and physical. Biology, botany, and zoology are examples of life sciences. Astronomy, chemistry, and geology are examples of physical sciences. One of the best ways to explore any of these branches is to build a school project. This could be for fun, or it could fulfill a class assignment. There's no better way to gain practical, hands-on experience than to create your school project in a makerspace.

Makerspaces are community-based workshops. They offer the safety, resources, and support to create anything from a pocket piano and robot to a smartphone microscope and articulated hand. Makerspaces are established in woodshops, auto shops, libraries, computer labs, and warehouses. They are found worldwide, and participation can be free or based on a paid membership.

Each makerspace is as unique as the do-it-yourself (DIY) users it serves. Participants include artists, hobbyists, teachers, students, entrepreneurs, and industry professionals. Although they may range in age and skill level, makers come together to explore project ideas, exchange know-how, and share designs. They also access a wide range of tools and equipment they wouldn't normally be able to use. Most makerspace have manual, power, and computer-controlled tools. Examples include hammers, saws, pliers, digital sewing machines, laser cutters, 3D printers, electronics, and metalworking equipment. How-to classes and workshops are often available. These teach beginning makers how to safely and effectively use the on-site equipment. Advanced classes dive deeper into detail and techniques. Makerspace amenities may include locker rooms, storage areas, a library of reference books, and display cases for finished projects.

Makerspaces encourage the blend of classroom knowledge and experimentation. Strategy, design, and the development of innovative solutions are all a part of the experience. In return, participants have fun creating, problem solving, moving beyond mistakes, and working with others. They learn how to think critically, manage time, and communicate effectively. New friends are made, and confidence soars. Plus, makers gain an impressive set of skills. These can open doors for higher education, a new career, or a money-making endeavor.

Every makerspace has an "if you can dream it, you can build it" mission. As you create, invent, and experiment, you will be well on your way to becoming an expert maker. And who knows, you may even develop a new method or technology to benefit the world around us.

CHAPTER ONE

LET THE SEWING BEGIN!

Bring artwork, fashion, and décor to life with LEDs, sensors, and microcontrollers. Each reacts to changes in the environment, allowing craft and science to mesh in a single spectacular project. To help you create these special effects, you will need a makerspace sewing machine.

A WORLD OF OPPORTUNITY WITH DIGITAL SEWING MACHINES

Three types of sewing machines can be found in makerspaces: mechanical, electronic, and computerized. They vary in ability but offer a world of opportunities for textile projects. Mechanical sewing machines are equipped with the basics: dials, knobs, levers, and switches. They run on electricity and are user controlled by hand. The stitches are made quickly but are not as precise as those made on electronic or computerized sewing machines.

Electronic sewing machines are the next step up. They feature a liquid crystal display (LCD) screen. This allows the user to select various decorative and utility stitches. Buttonholes and alphabets can also be created, depending on the model. They offer greater precision than a mechanical sewing machine.

High-tech digital sewing machines use advanced technology and multiple functions to help makers create textile projects. They can handle denim, satin, corduroy, and polyester fabrics easily.

Computerized sewing machines use internal micro-processors to control the automatic sewing. Decorative and utility stitches, as well as patterns, are saved on memory cards or cartridges. Some machines connect to a computer with internet access, allowing users to download even more stitches and patterns. Once the preferred stitches and patterns are entered into the machine, it will automatically create the design.

Additional tools and equipment are used to for textile projects. Irons remove deep wrinkles. Steamers freshen garments, curtains, and upholstery. Sergers sew, trim, and finish seams at the same time. Leather punches create holes in belts, watch straps, shoes, and saddles. Seam rippers pull out unwanted seams and attachments. And wooden hoops hold fabric for needlecraft.

THE MATERIALS LIST

Sewing machines work best with flexible materials, such as muslin, cotton, felt, leather, vinyl, and yarn. They can be sewn together, knotted, quilted, repaired, or altered. Regular thread is a common binder. However, there are other, more exciting materials, that will enhance a sewing project. These include conductive thread, programmable LEDs, and sewable circuits.

SAFETY MATTERS

Exercise caution when using a sewing machine. They are generally safe, but their needles have been known to pierce the skin if used carelessly. Always unplug any unused equipment.

TYPES OF MAKERSPACES

Makers have options when it comes to building projects: hackerspaces, makerspaces, Fab Labs, and TechShops. Hackerspaces or hacklabs were first established in the 1900s by European hacker club members who wanted to explore hardware and software capabilities. One of the earliest hacker clubs was c-base. It was established in Germany in 1995. Inspired, American hackers created their own spaces in 2007.

Makers at this 2015 Fab Lab Polytech area during PolyFest in St. Petersburg, Russia, gather together to promote knowledge, mentorship, and community.

Makerspaces are similar to hackerspaces. However, the *Makerspace Playbook*, 2nd ed makes this distinction: "Makerspaces focus primarily on learning and education, whereas hackerspaces often focus on hobbyists who make to have fun and relax, or who use the space as an incubator for their emerging small business." The term "makerspace" was first used by Dale Dougherty of Maker Media. He thought it was much more positive than "hacker," a term commonly used to describe those who use their computer skills to perform criminal acts.

Fab Lab users access laser cutters for multi-dimensional projects, milling machines for circuit boards, wood routers for furniture, vinyl cutters for flexible projects, and more. Fab Lab members stay connected by teaming up for projects and participating in workshops, video conferences, and annual meetings. Fab Labs offer either free or in-kind access to the public. Schools use them for science, technology, engineering, and math (STEM) projects.

For a fee, makers can use part-workshop, part-fabrication studios called TechShops. These locations offer on-hand staff to help with idea development and technical skills. TechShops also offer safety and basic use (SBU) classes to help new users learn how to safely operate equipment.

PROJECT 1: MAKE AN LED OCTOPUS USING CONDUCTIVE THREAD

Conductive thread and LEDs can turn an octopus into an impressive piece of art. It is based on the principles of electricity.

Electricity is a form of energy can be found in nature or made by rubbing two unlike items together, combining chemicals, or using a generator. In this case, electricity makes LEDs glow under flexible material. Conductive thread—a stainless steel fiber thread—conducts the electricity. It receives power from a coin battery and then transfers the power to the LEDs. Conductive thread should only be hand stitched, couched, or used in a sewing machine's bobbin. A computerized sewing machine is ideal for this project.

Necessary materials include fabrics in various colors and patterns, a large octopus outline, and a light box or makeshift light box (a flashlight under a glass table). Additional items include basting spray, conductive and glow-in-the-dark threads, LEDs, and a three-volt coin battery with its all-important polarity terminals—positive (+) and negative (-). A volt (V) is defined by WordCentral.com as:

> A unit of electrical potential difference and electro-motive force equal to the difference in potential between two points in a conducting wire carrying a constant current of one ampere when the power used between these two points is equal to one watt.

WHAT MAKES IT A GOOD SCIENCE PROJECT?

When choosing a science project, select something that goes beyond moldy bread and an erupting volcano. Your project will need to truly interest you. It will also need to follow the scientific method, an unbiased process used by scientists to highlight, observe, test, and share a problem.

The scientific method begins with a question. BrownDogGadgets.com's Wil Tushaus addresses this in his January 2016 article, "Solar Science Fair Project." He challenges students to not only ask a question, but to ask the right question. For example, a standard question for a solar science fair project could be, "Will this [homemade charger] charge my cell phone?" But this question can only bring a yes or no answer. This is very limiting. Tushaus offers some better questions, such as, "Which light source produces the best solar energy?" or "What is the best position to put a solar panel to collect energy?"

The scientific method can then continue by formulating a hypothesis, gathering the needed material, tools, and equipment, writing down

(continued on the next page)

(continued from the previous page)

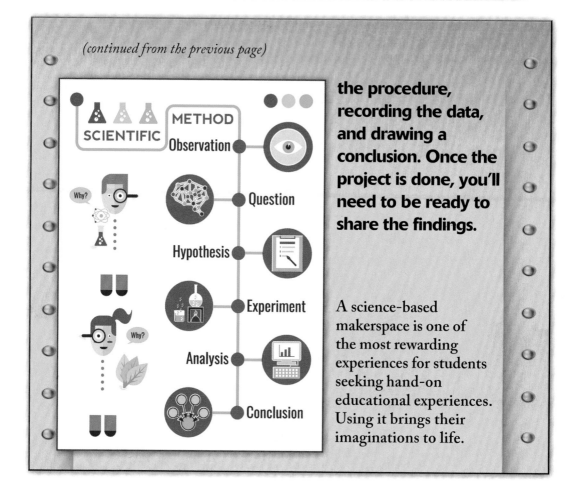

the procedure, recording the data, and drawing a conclusion. Once the project is done, you'll need to be ready to share the findings.

A science-based makerspace is one of the most rewarding experiences for students seeking hand-on educational experiences. Using it brings their imaginations to life.

The project involves cutting out the outline of the octopus. Place it against a contrasting fabric. Attach it to the fabric using stitches and basting spray. Then pin it to the couching. Sew it together with conductive thread. Attach battery terminals and LED lights.

CHAPTER TWO

CREATE CUTTING-EDGE PROJECTS

A lthough it resembles a printer, a laser cutter is far more complex than one. It depends on software to render vector drawings and uses an invisible laser to vaporize materials. The laser cutter makes quick, precise cuts in wood, paper, acrylic, felt, and cardboard. The resulting cutout can then be assembled into a 3D structure. Clocks, helicopter models, wooden eyeglasses, and bendable books—there's no limit to what this machine can make!

SAFETY MATTERS

A laser cutter is housed in a cabinet container. Inside, interlocks and safety systems prevent the laser from escaping. If the lid or access panels are opened during operation, the machine will shut down immediately. Plus, the glass topper will filter out damaging rays. However, it's always a good idea to wear safety goggles when operating the laser cutter. You may also want to wear a mask over your mouth as you may be exposed to irritating fumes. Most laser cutters come with an air filter and/or are linked to an outdoor vent.

The most common laser cutter hazard is that it will catch fire. If this occurs, reach for a carbon dioxide (CO_2) or halon fire extinguisher. One of these should be positioned nearby. The first removes oxygen from the

To safely operate a laser cutter, it is always a good idea to take a class taught by an instructor or a trained volunteer.

fire, which is effective but messy. The second is a residue-free fire extinguisher containing gas. It is used to protect electrical equipment from burning fuels.

PROJECT 2: EXPLORING MOBILE FORCES

Art and engineering come together when making a mobile. Mobiles are hanging or suspended structures that should

The mobile was created by Pennsylvania-native Alexander Calder (1898–1976). He studied mechanical engineering and later worked as a sculptor in Paris, France.

remain balanced. If they are affected by a force, they will then return to rest. Forces are the push or pull applied to a particular object. Physicist and mathematician Isaac Newton considered this in his first law, "An object in motion will remain in motion and an object at rest will remain at rest unless acted upon by an unbalanced force." Forces affect a great many things. Take, for instance, the forces of gravity, weather, people, furniture, and cars on buildings and bridges. Architects and engineers consider all of these forces when designing structures.

CONNECT TO A MAKERSPACE

Makerspaces are located in communities around the world. You can find them online using websites such as The Makers Nation. This organization is based in Ontario, Canada. Its mission is to expose makers to "crazy-awesome maker activities happening in their cities." These take place across North America and in cities such as Singapore. The Makers Nation also hosts events. Another similar event is Maker Faire. Hosted by Maker Media, it is a worldwide "show and tell." The first Maker Faire was held in 2006 in San Mateo, California. Makers presented projects, and curious attendees came to check them out. It was a huge hit and spurred other Maker Faires in hundreds of locations around the globe. Flagship Maker Faires, which are produced by the Maker Media team, take place in the San Francisco Bay Area in California, and in New York City. Feature Faires take place in regional locations, including Madrid, Tokyo, Istanbul, Stockholm, and Rome. Mini Maker Faires pop up across the world in communities, including Bangkok, Bogota, Kiev, Jerusalem, and Vancouver. School Maker Faires are specifically for K–12 students and are family-friendly events that celebrate the maker movement. For more information, visit MakerFaire.com.

Makers go through a similar process when crafting mobiles. On a smaller scale, they balance the forces of gravity and convection (the movement of air currents). Makers want to make sure their design can hold and balance the weight of its objects. If a person were to pull on an object, it would have potential or stored energy. Once released, the object's potential energy would become kinetic energy—energy produced because it's in motion. If no additional forces were applied, the mobile would eventually regain its balance and return to rest.

Explore forces by making a mobile. You can use construction paper and string, or make it more sophisticated with laser-cut structures and durable cord. You can then make a modified two-piece hanger, or cross boards, from which to hang the structures. These two pieces will need to have a hole drilled into the middle of each piece. After being arranged perpendicularly (one vertical and one horizontal), the pieces can be strung together. The objects—which can also be laser cut in various sizes and shapes—are then hung at differing lengths with more durable cord. Aim for balance and visual interest. An instructor or staff person can help you download the necessary computer files and operate the laser cutter. Depending on your science interests, you may want to expound on the mobile. For example, if you're studying astronomy, structures could be cut to represent stars and planets.

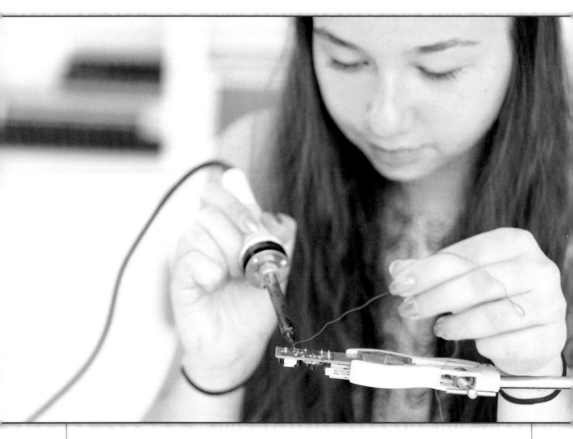

Soldering is safe with these precautions: seek instruction before you begin, and always wash your hands after. You'll also need clamps to hold components in place and a resting stand.

PROJECT 3: LIGHT IT UP WITH A SOLAR SCIENCE STATION

For billions of years, the sun has been producing a usable power known as energy. When the sun's rays, containing energy, reach Earth, the energy is transformed into heat and electricity. Solar energy does not pollute water or air, nor does it produce greenhouse gases that lead to global warming and climate change. According to the US Energy Information Administration:

> The amount of solar energy that the earth receives each day is many times greater than the total amount of energy consumed around the world. However, on the surface of the earth, solar energy is a variable and intermittent energy source. The amount of sunlight and the intensity of sunlight varies by location. Weather and climate conditions affect the availability of sunlight on a daily and seasonal basis. The type and size of a solar energy collection and conversion system determines how much of available solar energy can be converted into useful energy.

Explore solar power energy by building your own solar science station. You will be able to record data, as well as plug in a mobile device, appliance, or even an Arduino project with the USB output and power-out terminals. This version requires soldering, but you can purchase a nonsoldering kit online. Solder is a mix of melted metals that are used to join metallic surfaces. A soldering iron is used to melt solder.

To begin, gather together plywood, a 5.5V 320mA solar cell, a USB charging circuit, blue LEDs, and stranded and solid core wires. The tools needed include scissors, screwdrivers, and wire strippers. An instructor or fellow maker can guide you through the assembly. Or you can search online for additional instructions.

Use your solar science station to charge three rechargeable AA batteries. Simply place them into the battery holder, put the station in the direct sunlight, and switch the holder to the on position. Wait approximately three days. An LED voltmeter will indicate whether or not the batteries are fully charged. One rechargeable AA has the potential for 1.2 to 1.25 volts. Multiply this by three, and you will have about 3.6 to 3.75 volts of power.

Once charged, you can either plug in a USB device, or start using your solar science station for science. Put it in direct sunlight, and begin recording solar energy measurements each day and at the same time. You can also determine whether or not the angle (0, 45, or 90 degrees) or the facing (north, south, east, and west) of a solar panel alters its voltage output.

CHAPTER THREE

EASY AS 1-2-3D!

A 3D Printer is one of the most popular tools in the makerspace. It transforms digital designs into complex physical objects. You can create phone cases, platform sandals, a dinosaur shower head, or even something that has never before existed.

HOW IT WORKS

Traditional printers work in 2D, meaning they create along two space measurements: X for the horizontal axis, and Y for the vertical axis. 3D printers, on the other hand, work with X-Y-Z axes. Using computer programs, you can move, rotate, and scale objects on the screen. Copy and adjust these simple shapes to create variations, then add new shapes to increase the project complexity.

SOFTWARE MAKES IT EASY

To begin, you'll need to design your project as a digital 3D design file using computer-aided design (CAD) software. CAD lets you build a collection of parts, make changes easily, reuse design components, and simulate designs without the trouble of constructing a physical prototype. Designs become digital files, which are the blueprints for creating your physical object. The design file is then transformed into thin layers, which are sent to a 3D printer. Technology then determines the printing process.

23

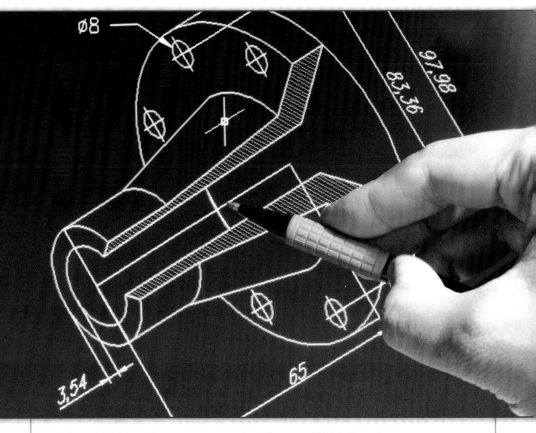

A knowledge of computer-aided design (CAD) software can open up a wide variety of professional opportunities. This software is used in architecture, art, drafting, and engineering.

Some CAD applications (apps) are free, while others need to be purchased. Autodesk is a popular CAD software brand. It features 123-D, a suite of software that can be downloaded for free. If you're a beginner, learn about 3D modeling and printing with Autodesk's Tinkercad. If you're more advanced, their other apps may be more your speed.

You can render 3D models from favorite photos using 123D Catch. Design electronic projects using 123D Circuits. Turn any 3D model into a 3D puzzle with 123D. Create 3D sculptures on an iPad using 123D Sculpt+.

THE MATERIALS LIST

A 3D printer uses a variety of materials, depending on the brand and model. Materials vary, ranging from rubber and sandstone to ceramics and metals. There are also two types of plastics that are used: acrylonitrile butadiene styrene (ABS) and polylactic acid (PLA).

ABS is strong, flexible, and resilient. It is the same plastic that Lego uses. ABS is quick and easy to print. The plastic starts to soften at 221°F (105°C). This makes a difference if you plan to print something that would be set in high temperatures. Examples include coasters for hot drinks or a dashboard decoration that could be in a hot car. However, once it's been extruded, it will shrink as it cools. This can lead to cracking, splitting, or lifting from the bed. To prevent drastic changes, print in a location that is not too cold or drafty. ABS is often used for wearable projects and for those items that could be dropped, roughed up, or used in hot temperatures. Items include cases for mobile devices, wedding rings, and tool handles.

PLA is a bioplastic, which means that it can be recycled or composted. PLA is sticky, expanding as it melts. A drop of oil can be added for smooth printing. Unlike ABS, PLA has very little shrinkage. You can print larger jobs, such as models

The inside of a vehicle can be hot and damage some materials. Makers should choose the materials they use wisely.

and boxes, without fear of lifting, cracking, or warping. PLA is even an ideal material for printing outdoor projects, such as garden décor, because it's insoluble in water. If you plan to put your PLA project in temperatures greater than 140°F (60°C), you may want to use a different material. PLA sags in high heat. It is also brittle, making it a poor choice for objects that tend to be dropped, such as tool handles.

PATENTS AND INTELLECTUAL PROPERTY

You can make almost anything in a makerspace, but that doesn't mean you should. Some designs, patterns, and models are protected by patents. Patents are property rights, granted by a government, to the owner of the patent. Patents prevent others from using, duplicating, altering, or selling the finished product. Patents are valid for a specific number of years and are only recognized in the issuing country. Makers who want to secure patents in other countries must apply in each individual country.

If you want to craft, build, or print another's project, check the licensing agreement put in place by the designer. This is often noted in the design specifications. Thingiverse offers a Creative Commons (CC) license, allowing submitters to share their 3D designs. Makers can then use, further develop, or remix the designs. This fosters collaboration within the maker community. Submitters can also choose whether attribution (crediting the creator) should be required and whether the completed project can be sold for profit. When makers download an item from Thingiverse, they must adhere to the type of license selected by the creator.

(continued on the next page)

27

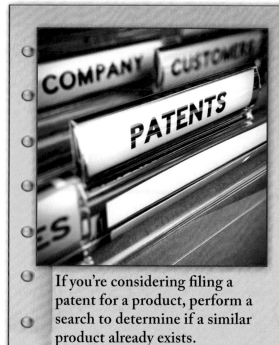

(continued from the previous page)

If you use, duplicate, alter, or sell a patented design without the permission of the patent owner, you could be infringing on intellectual property. The patent owner could sue you in federal court, and if found guilty, you may be ordered to pay monetary damages.

If you're considering filing a patent for a product, perform a search to determine if a similar product already exists.

ON-DEMAND PRINTING

Extrusion-based printers build 3D projects, layer after layer. Objects can be manufactured on a small scale. Plastic material is melted and laid down, one layer at a time, onto a print platform. This allows users to print objects on their own and as often as needed. The printing speed depends on the amount of plastic needed for each project. Hollow objects, such as whistles, need less plastic and less time.

If you don't have a desktop 3D printer, consider using a large industrial machine. You can send your designs to a service provider, such as i.Materialise, Ponoko, or Shapeways. For a fee, they will use larger production capabilities to print your digital design using your choice of material and finish. The object will be then be shipped to you.

Other option is to use 3D Hubs, the Amsterdam-based company that connects makers who need to have their projects printed with those who own 3D printers. 3D Hubs operates in more than 160 countries and uses matchmaking algorithms to note the best 3D print options for their projects, offering 3D-printing services within ten miles (sixteen kilometers) of their home. This is particularly helpful for prototypes and small production items.

SAFETY MATTERS

Generally, 3D printers are very safe, especially if located in an open and/or well-ventilated location. The print extruder, also known as the print head, heats up to several hundred degrees. It is located internally and should not be touched. When printing, a slight "hot plastic" smell may fill the space. This is normal, but you may experience irritation of the eyes and lungs.

PROJECT 4: SHAKE, RATTLE, AND EARTHQUAKE

Thousands of earthquakes rattle the globe each day—some you can feel, but most you don't. An earthquake is a sudden, and sometimes violent, adjustment of the earth's tectonic plates. These plates are like puzzle pieces. They constantly move slowly past one another. The edges, known as plate boundaries, are made up of many faults. Most of the world's

Many seismologists work in the oil and petroleum industries, but others study earthquakes and their effects.

earthquakes occur on these faults. The edges are rough and get stuck. All the while, the plates continue to move. When the plates move far enough, the edges unstick, resulting in an earthquake. This produces a force that builds until the crust breaks. Stress is then released as energy, moving through the Earth in the form of ripple-like waves called seismic waves. These waves have been known to travel hundreds of miles to the Earth's surface. We feel them in the form of an earthquake.

Immediately after an earthquake hits, scientists rate the strength and duration of its seismic waves. A rating of 3-5 is minor or light; 5-7 is moderate to strong, 7-8 is major, and 8 or higher is great. Scientists also create shakemaps. The US Geological Survey (USGS) archives shakemaps from all over the world.

Turn your earthquake interest into a 3D topographic map. To begin, visit USGS.gov to download a ShakeMap for the earthquake of your choice. You will need QGIS—a geographic information system (GIS) application—to view the shapefiles. From the various downloaded shapefiles, you will use the peak ground velocity (PGV) shapefile to view the shake contours.

When it's time to print, you'll load the file into 3D-printing software. Because topography is stacked straight up, supports won't be needed. You will, however, need a large, flat base. Just be careful as the print may lift from the base as it prints. PLA is recommened.

PROJECT 5: BIG LEARNING WITH 3D MOLECULES

Proteins are long chain-like molecules made by the cells in our bodies. This process is called protein synthesis. There are thousands of types of proteins in our bodies, each with a specific function to keep us alive. Structural proteins, such as collagen for connective tissue like tendons and ligaments, give structure to our bodies. Transport proteins, such as hemoglobin for oxygen distribution, carry important nutrients through body parts. Catalysts, such as enzymes for digestion, jump-start chemical reactions. And defensive proteins, also known as antibodies, ward off disease-causing bacteria and toxins.

Create your own 3D structure of a protein.

To begin, install the programming language Python. You won't be coding, but it's used by the modeling and visualization program, PyMOL. Install PyMOL. Now it's time to pick a protein. The Research Collaboratory for Structural Bioinformatics (RCSB) is a useful resource. When scientists discover new protein structures, they submit them to online repositories, such as the RCSB. Scientists, as well as the general public, can then access the proteins for study. The RCSB keeps an archive that is filled with a wide variety. It even features a protein of the month, along with 3D models, write-ups, and animations to describe the function and significance of the protein. Download the 3D structure, and view it by opening the file in PyMOL. Then print your chosen protein via your makerspace 3D printer.

CHAPTER FOUR

ELECTRONICS

Electricity is created by the movement of electrons. Energy is produced, which can be harnessed to create a charge. Charges power light bulbs, air conditioners, video gaming systems, electric cars, and many other things.

HOW IT WORKS

To understand electronics, one must understand its building blocks: voltage (volts or V), currents (amperes or A), and resistance (omega or ohm). Working with electricity means working with two points. One of these points always has a greater charge than the other. That difference is called voltage. The rate at which the charge flows is known as current. Resistance is the material's tendency to resist the electrical current. When discussing these values, we're really talking about the movement of charge and ultimately the behavior of electrons.

When working with electronics, makers build electric circuits. These pathways are made of wire through which electrons flow. A power source provides voltage, causing the electrons to move, and thus power up a device. For example, a simple circuit can cause a light to blink or a gadget to play your favorite tune.

This action is controlled by a microcontroller. These tiny, but powerful, computers are on a single integrated circuit, also known as a computer chip. They are commonly used in everything from keyboards

33

Computer chips—integrated circuits that process information— are made with pure silicon crystal.

and modems to printers and vehicles. You can code microcontrollers to perform actions, such as measuring, calculating, and displaying information. There are two ways to use a microcontroller. Use a microcontroller motherboard or integrate a microcontroller on a circuit board (temporarily or permanently with soldering). The former is the easiest for beginners, and the most popular microcontroller motherboard is Arduino (pronounced ar-DWEE-no).

LEARNING WITH ARDUINO

Arduino is an open-source microcontroller board—a simple computer—that runs a simple program over and over again. Makers write code in Arduino's software, which tells the microcontroller what to do. Arduino is powered by batteries (regular or solar) or electricity from an electrical wall socket. Arduino is easy to build and modify, allowing you to make all sorts of interactive toys, tools, gadgets, and robots. You can even program Arduino to send a Tweet when your morning coffee is ready.

To make a basic Arduino, you'll need an oscilloscope to monitor voltage and the continuity of an electrical circuit. You'll also need a soldering iron to attach components and wires to a circuit board. Additional tools include wire cutters and wire strippers. Eventually you'll learn how to design your own circuit boards. This will enable you to create more advanced projects, such as robots and mobile devices. More complex electronics include robotics, which calls for more advanced tools and problem-solving skills.

Arduino Uno is the most common type of microcontroller motherboard. Mega's slightly larger circuit board follows Arduino Uno in popularity. It comes with a 256 KB of memory, eight times more than that of Arduino Uno. Arduino Mega ADK is a specialized version of Arduino Mega. It interfaces with Android devices. Arduino LilyPad uses conductive thread and is specifically designed for textile projects.

ADVANCING TO RASPBERRY PI

If you plan to build a more complicated project or one that performs more than a single task, you'll need Raspberry Pi. Raspberry Pi is a general-purpose computer that uses a Linux operating system. It's a bit more complicated than Arduino, but just as fun, and even more functional. Examples of Raspberry Pi projects include an automated cat feeder and

Raspberry Pi is a great introduction to the world of computing. Students can use this mini computer to learn and experiment with hardware, coding, and programming their own projects.

a tea kettle activator that measures water temperatures before lowering the tea into the kettle for brewing.

When determining whether to use Arduino or Raspberry Pi for your project idea, consider the rule of thumb offered by Patrick Di Justo of Makezine.com. He wrote, "Think about what you want your project to do. If you can describe it with less than two 'and's, get an Arduino. If you need more than two 'and's, get a Raspberry Pi." Di Justo continues by offering this example:

"I want to monitor my plants and have them Tweet me when they need water." That can best be done by an Arduino. "I want to monitor my plants and have them Tweet me when they need water and check the National Weather Service and, if the forecast is for fair weather, turn on the irrigation system and if the forecast is for rain, do nothing." That would best be handled by a Raspberry Pi.

SAFETY MATTERS

Electronics at this level are low powered and are considered safe. In general, care should be taken when working with any materials (batteries, circuit boards, and sensors) and tools (wire strippers, stands, and vacuums). Working with electronics often requires soldering. In general, solder contains lead. Although it does not present a health risk, it's always a good idea to wash your hands after working with the material for a long period of time. You can also use a lead-free solder, but it is difficult to work with. Lead-free solder requires higher soldering temperatures. It also produces toxic fumes and corrodes soldering tips. Regardless of your choice, be sure to work in a well-ventilated area. Use caution when working with soldering irons as they can reach approximately 400°F (204°C).

PROJECT 6: STAR CHARTS POWERED BY ARDUINO

Star charts, or star maps, are used to navigate the sky. They feature the brightest stars (spheres of hot gas) and constellations (groups of stars) as seen from the Earth. And now you can make your own star chart. The project calls for WS2812B LEDs and Arduino Uno, which controls each LED individually in order to showcase a particular constellation.

Additional items include a 5V power supply, press board, flat black spray paint, aluminum foil, a silver-colored Sharpie marker, and an adhesive (hot glue, packing tape, or duct tape). A drill with at least three bits of various sizes will be needed to punch holes in the press board. These will be used for the stars. A router can be used to create a border around the stars. After applying a coat of flat black spray paint, you can put the LEDs in place and let the constellations wow your teachers and classmates!

Blow Your Mind with Lego® Mindstorms

Lego Mindstorms kits are used to teach skills to people of all ages and interests. Elementary students use them to learn programming. Middle schoolers use them to learn automation. High schoolers use them to discover robotics. And college students use them as an introduction to engineering. Even industry professionals use Lego Mindstorms for research projects.

Lego Mindstorms EV3 is a robotic set that lets you build and program your own robot. The website Lego.com offers easy-to-follow steps to help you build robots that do everything from walk and spin to shoot and slither. The site features a Lego Robot Mak3r Studio, in which you can see what other EV3 fans have developed. The EV3 Programmer App lets you choose your robot. It also offers building instructions and a programming tool. The EV3 Brick functions as the robot's control center and power station. The Videos subpage offers how-to tutorials, fan spotlights, and inspiration for those looking for their next school project. Lego welcomes innovation and has set up an online builder community in which creations can be shared. Makers can visit lego.com for inspiration for every interest and skill level.

PROJECT 7: DIY ROBOTS

Robots are among the most popular makerspace projects to create. To make your own, connect with a makerspace in your school or community today.

Robots have long fascinated people. Books have been written about them, movies tell of their exploits, and now makers create them to impress teachers, classmates, and science fair attendees. Robots come in all shapes and sizes and are used in many industries, including education, entertainment, manufacturing, and science. They are categorized as ground robots with fixed arms, humanoids, rovers, turtles, and walkers. They can also be aerial vehicles or underwater robots. Robots can function automatically or be controlled by computer.

Students who are interested in robotics are encouraged to begin with circuit-based analog robots. Electronic circuitry causes them to move and be controlled using a wired remote controller.

The first turtle robots, Elmer and Elsie, and underwater remotely operated vehicles (ROVs) are analog robots. But don't be intimidated by these projects. Kits are available with the circuit design already in place. You can also build your own. This project helps you create an obstacle-avoiding, wall-follower robot that is controlled by a smartphone. Among the materials needed are Arduino Uno, a gear motor, wheels, 9V batteries, and a plastic box. You'll also need a soldering iron, hot glue gun, screwdriver, and drill.

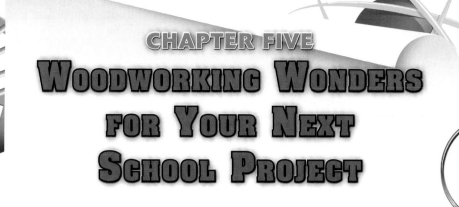

CHAPTER FIVE

WOODWORKING WONDERS FOR YOUR NEXT SCHOOL PROJECT

Long-lasting, attractive, and easy to find, wood continues to be a favorite makerspace material. It comes in a variety of colors, grains, weights, patterns, and textures. Wood can be cut, shaped, and painted to make containers, cutouts, and stands for science-based school

Woodworking is fun and rewarding for students of all ages and skill levels. Makers enjoy the process of creating meaningful projects.

projects. To work with wood, you'll need an assortment of manual and powered tools. These include hammers, screwdrivers, saws, sanders, chisels, routers, and drill presses.

SAFETY MATTERS

Wear gloves and safety glasses or goggles at all times to prevent cuts, splinters, and debris from flying into your eyes. A respirator will keep dust and fumes from entering breathing passages. Earplugs or earmuffs should be worn when working with extremely loud power tools. (A noise reduction rating or NRR will ensure optimal protection for your hearing.) Finally, long hair and loose clothing should be secured into place in order to avoid getting caught in machinery.

WHERE TO FIND INSPIRATION

Project inspiration is all around—online, in-print, or at special maker events. Thingiverse and Shapeways are two of the many online sources for all things "3D printer." Makers can search from the nearly one million 3D models that have been uploaded onto Thingiverse.com. Hundreds of free lessons are also available. Users can "like" a model, comment, and share their own version of an already-published project. Shapeways features a 3D-parts database with free files that

(continued on the next page)

(continued from the previous page)

have been "tried and tested" by other users. You offer feedback, and even upload your own designs and products. Instructables.com offers web-based documentation for maker members. Since 2005, it has published over one hundred thousand projects. Explore a wealth of project categories, from technology and craft to food and costumes. Enter contests, join a group, comment in a forum, ask questions, or share your own projects with its ever-growing community. For a fee, you can take one of Instructables.com's classes.

Some sources share ideas that are specific to their materials. The online company littleBits sells magnetic components that snap together to make just about anything you can think of—minus any complicated programming, soldering, or wires! Create your own project, or order project-specific kits from littleBits.cc. Kit examples include a remote control, a remote-controlled pet feeder, and an analog synthesizer. In fact, littleBits was highlighted in another great project resource: *Make* magazine (Vol. 44, April/May 2015). This subscription-based periodical showcases fun-filled projects, tutorials, and reviews for makers, regardless of skill level. Instructions, time required, cost, materials, and tools are listed along with full-color images.

PROJECT 8: A "HANDY" PROJECT

The human hand is intricate. It uses twenty-nine bones and thirty-four muscles to perform everyday activities, such as writing, gripping a soda can, and playing a video game. Articulated hands make for a fun physical science project. To make your own, you'll need hardwood dowels, pine planks, braided nylon string, and sheet rock screws. Necessary tools include a small drill press, side grinder, jig saw (or saber saw), and a chop saw with a trim blade. To begin, draw and cut out a hand template. The template will then transfer to the pine planks. Wooden shapes will need to be cut out to make the hand, finger bone segments, and joints. Nylon string will mimic the function of ligaments, which connect bones and cartilage. It will also mimic tendons, which attach muscles to bones.

For additional learning, draw the physiology of the hand and forearm on the articulated hand. Include the bones of the fingers (phalanges, metacarpals, and carpals), as well as the bones of the forearm (radius and ulna). Use paint to darken the negative space. Light paint can be used for the bones. You can label the bones, and use different colors of nylon string to distinguish ligaments from tendons. To further challenge your makerspace skills, try upgrading the wood and nylon string to copper water pipe, soldered joints, and muscle memory wire.

MAKE MONEY WITH YOUR MAKERSPACE SKILLS

Many makers have used their skills to make some extra cash. Some create original, customized products to sell on creative online marketplaces, such as Etsy and Quirky. Makers subscribe by setting up online stores. They pay listing and transaction fees and are able to access helpful support, education, and management tools. Other makers sell unique products on crowdfunding sites such as Indiegogo and Kickstarter. Crowdfunding refers to online funding platforms that invite visitors to finance projects they would like to see in production. These investors then contribute a small amount of money toward the project. The more money that is pledged, the greater the chance a product can make it through the production process. The crowd-sourcing option helps makers turn their ideas into reality without incurring business debt, provided enough money is raised.

PROJECT 9: IT'S A BIRD, IT'S A PLANE, IT'S AN AIR TRAJECTORY

According to Merriam-Webster's online dictionary, a trajectory is "the curved path along which something (such as a rocket) moves through the air or through space." Trajectories

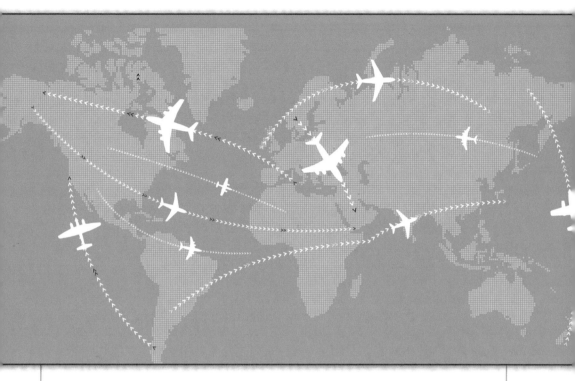

Everything from balls to stuffed animals to bullets and airplanes follow trajectories. Two forces affect trajectories: inertia that sends the objects flying and gravity that sends the objects down.

are often studied in physics. Physics examines the interaction of matter and energy and what they experience when in contact with electricity, heat, light, and sound. Students interested in physics can enter an annual competition called the Science Olympiad. This competition has various levels. The Elementary Science Olympiad (ESO) program is for students in kindergarten through sixth grade. The Science Olympiad is a little different. It's for sixth to twelfth graders who join school-based teams. Students prepare year-round for a variety of hands-on events in all sorts of sciences, including anatomy, chemistry, earth science, genetics, geology, mechanical engineering, physics, and technology.

One of the Science Olympiad events is Air Trajectory. Participants are required to build a device that uses the gravitational energy of a falling mass to directly or indirectly launch a projectile. For example, a weight that is dropped on an apparatus will cause a ball to shoot out of it like a bullet. To qualify, the air trajectory must meet special requirements, including building specs, measurements, and safety protection for set up and operation.

To make your own air trajectory, you'll need a wood block to be dropped on a two-liter bottle, thus launching a ping-pong ball across the room. Materials include plywood, PVC pipe, fittings, pipe clamps, and tape. Tools, such as a saw, drill press, and screw drivers, are also needed. Instructions can be found online or by reaching out to your makerspace community.

CHAPTER SIX

MIX IT UP WITH METALWORKING

Unique jewelry pieces, aluminum dice, stainless steel roses, fine chain mail, ice ball makers, and replacement car parts—you can create all of these and more with metalworking. You'll need to use a great deal of focus, strength, and the ability to work with high temperatures. As you begin to learn the skill, hand tools will be used to fashion small projects. Power tools can be added as skills improve, allowing you to fabricate larger, more complex projects.

SAFETY MATTERS

Flying debris is common when working with metal. To avoid injury, safety glasses, hearing protection, and gloves are recommended. Cuff-less pants and high-top shoes are always a good idea, and if you plan to work with a torch or welder, be sure to wear goggles, heat-resistant gloves, a face shield, and sleeved bibs offer extra protection. A face mask will also protect you from flying debris, as well as prevent fume inhalation.

PROJECT 10: EXPLORING AFTERIMAGES

Colored afterimages are optical illusions that are seen after staring at an original image. They are also known as ghost images."They commonly occur after staring at a bright light for a long period of time. This is true if one stares at color. Cone cells in your eyes work together to help perceive variants in color. Cone cells are small and are shaped like cones. They are located on the retina at the back of the eye. They come in three types: red, blue, and green. Each is sensitive to red, blue, and green, and allow us to see combinations of these colors. All three are needed to see colors properly. For example, the red cones are stimulated when you look at a red stop sign. The red cones alert your brain the sign is red. The various cone cells work together, helping you to see a vibrant world of color. Colors other than the three primary colors are mixtures of red, blue, and green. For example, purple is a mixture of red and blue. Thus, the red and blue cone cells are activated. The color white occurs when all three primary colors are mixed together as all three cone types are encouraged to see white light.

However, afterimages appear when you stare at a color image for thirty seconds. The cone cells get tired and take a brief break. For example, you can stare at a red image, look at a white space, and immediately see an afterimage. This afterimage may mimic the original image in size and shape, but it will be bluish green. This occurs because the red cone cells are fatigued. They cannot detect red. Within a few seconds, however, they will recover. The afterimage will disappear, replaced by the white colors.

When the primary color mixtures occur, secondary colors will appear. For example, green and blue produces cyan, while red and green produces yellow. The longer one focuses on a single color, the longer the afterimage will stick. This is because the cone cells need a bit more time to recover.

You can explore the biology behind this occurrence with an afterimages project. It can be simple with just a few materials to gather: a stop watch, colored pencils, a piece of paper, a computer, and a color monitor. You'll also need participants to join you. They will stare at the white spot on the colored circle for thirty seconds as you time them, using the stopwatch. Then they will need to immediately turn their eyes to the white space. Using the colored pencils, they can then draw the afterimages they see on the paper.

With metalworking, you can expand or modify this activity. Cut metal pieces, and solder them onto a color wheel. Or add an electrical component, and fabricate a large street lamp with red, blue, and green lights. Build a frame for a poster or piece of cloth to act as a white space. Continue exploring by noting the time it takes for each color's afterimage to disappear. Experiment with other colors. You can also use this project to discuss color blindness, the condition of the eyes when their cones do not properly identify colors.

If you're ready to give wings to your "big idea,"

The color circle was developed by Sir Isaac Newton in 1666. Color wheels include a range from primary to mixed colors.

CREATE YOUR OWN MAKERSPACE

Can't find a makerspace in your community? Start your own. First consider a good location that is well ventilated, provides access to electricity, and can be securely locked up. An internet connection is bonus. Perhaps your school has an available woodshop, auto shop, art studio, or home economics room. Or you can turn to local community spaces, such as public libraries, art centers, science centers, and museums. These can be high-profile locations and should attract new and existing makers in the area. Once in your makerspace, outfit it with tables that will invite makers to lay out tools and project components. Add books, newspapers, and magazines for easy-access inspiration. Next consider supplying power tools, computers, and electronic equipment.

Safety is most important. Always keep a first aid kit clearly marked and accessible. You will also want to provide a way to call 911 in the event of an emergency. Also, makers tend to get messy, so it's important to have clean-up tools and products in a handy location. Be sure to provide some sort of storage in the event makers want to store projects that are in progress. Proper ventilation is

also needed. You'll also need to provide sufficient space for activities and storage. Insurance may need to be purchased to cover makers and their guests should an accident occur. Be sure to post the safety rules for each station in an easy-to-read location. And if protective gear if provided, be sure that everyone is aware and has access to it. For additional makerspace ideas, or ways to improve a favorite makerspace, check out Makerspace.com's *The Makerspace Playbook*, 2nd ed.

take advantage of what a local makerspace has to offer. Let creativity and collaboration help bring your project to completion. You'll find that your new skills will increase your science know-how, boost your confidence, and better our world.

alloy A mixture of two or more metals, or a metal with a nonmetal.

bobbin A cylinder-shaped object on a sewing machine that holds thread.

conductive thread A special kind of cotton or polyester thread that carries electrical current due to the addition of alloys of conductive materials (silver, copper, tin, and nickel).

couched To secure a thread by fastening it with a string of small stitches.

entrepreneur One who starts a business, and assumes all responsibility for its management, operation, and financial obligations.

fabrication The process used to manufacture a product.

generator A machine designed to produce electricity.

global warming A slow increase of the Earth's temperature, which is believed to be the cause of a permanent climate change.

greenhouse gases Compounds, such as carbon dioxide (CO_2) and methane (CH_4), that trap heat in the Earth's atmosphere.

hacker A computer enthusiast who legally (or illegally) works and experiments with computer hardware and software.

hypothesis An assumption that has yet to be proven.

infringe To overstep one's boundaries in order to trespass on another's rights or privileges.

insoluble The inability of a substance to dissolve in a liquid; the opposite of soluble.

interlocks An arrangement of one part that prevents another part from loosening.

microprocessors Tiny computer processors that are located on an integrated-circuit chip.

open source A program-sharing approach in which users are free to use, modify, and redistribute designs.

plywood Material that is made up of thin sheets of wood that have been glued in adjacent layers for strength and durability.

polarity The condition of having to opposite charges, positive and negative, in one location.

projectile An object that is released into the air with force.

prototype The first version of an object that is later reproduced or copied.

render To cause to be.

serge To prevent the fraying of material by adding extra stitches.

sewable circuits Circuits that can be attached to soft material via needle and thread.

topographic A map that displays the features of a particular area of land.

vaporize To convert something into vapors.

vector A quantity, often represented by a line segment, that has both magnitude and direction.

wire strippers A tool that removes electrical insulation from a wire tip.

FIRST
200 Bedford Street
Manchester, NH 03101
(800) 871-8326
Website: http://www.firstinspires.org
FIRST takes STEM education to a new level, encouraging
hands-on engineering through robotics in grade schools
across the United States.

FIRST Robotics Canada
PO Box 518
Pickering Main
Pickering, ON L1V 2R7
Canada
Website: http://www.firstroboticscanada.org
FIRST Robotics Canada is the charitable arm of US FIRST.
It supports FIRST Robotics teams in Canada.

Let's Talk Science
1584 North Routledge Park
London, ON N6H 5L6
Canada
+1 (877) 474-4081
Website: http://www.letstalkscience.ca
Let's Talk Science is a charitable organization based in
Canada that is committed to inspiring and engaging
Canadian students to get involved in STEM.

MakerKids
2451 Bloor Street W
Toronto, ON M6S 1P7
Canada
+1 (647) 247-1678
Website: http://www.makerkids.ca
MakerKids hosts programs that empower young makers to be
    creators, and not just consumers. STEM topics include
    coding, minecraft, and robotics.

Maker Media, Inc.
1005 Gravenstein Highway North
Sebastopol, CA 95472
Website: http://makermedia.com
As a driving force behind the makerspace movement,
    Maker Media offers media, events and ecommerce,
    namely *Make:* magazine, Maker Faire, Maker Shed,
    and Makezine.com.

Thingiverse
MakerBot Industries, LLC
One MetroTech Center, 21st Floor
Brooklyn, NY 11201
Website: http://www.thingiverse.com
Thingiverse produces 3D printers and provides the world's
    largest 3D-printing community in which makers can
    share designs.

Vocademy
1635 Spruce Street
Riverside, CA 92507
(951) 266-6630
Website: http://www.vocademy.com
Vocademy is an education-focused makerspace. It offers
school shop classes, trade schools, R&D labs, and
dream garages, as well as beginner-to-expert classes
for kids, employees, teachers, students, organizations,
and companies.

WEBSITES

Because of the changing nature of internet links, Rosen
Publishing has developed an online list of websites related to
the subject of this book. This site is updated regularly. Please
use this link to access this list:

http://www.rosenlinks.com/UMFSP/science

Cohen, Jacob. *Getting the Most Out of Makerspaces to Build Robots*. New York, NY: Rosen Publishing, 2015.

Editors of Brain Quest. *Everything You Need to Ace Science in One Big Fat Notebook: The Complete Middle School Study Guide*. New York, NY: Workman Publishing Company, 2016.

Graves, Colleen and Aaron Graves. *The Big Book of Makerspace Projects: Inspiring Makers to Experiment, Create, and Learn*. New York, NY: McGraw-Hill Education TAB, 2016.

Hackett, Chris and the Editors of Popular Science. *The Big Book of Maker Skills (Popular Science): Tools & Techniques for Building Great Tech Projects*. San Francisco, CA: Weldon Owen, 2014.

Petrikowski, Nicki Peter. *Getting the Most Out of Makerspaces to Create with 3-D Printers*. New York, NY: Rosen Publishing, 2015.

Preddy, Leslie B. *School Library Makerspaces: Grades 6-12*. Santa Barbara, CA: ABC-CLIO, LLC, 2013.

Rauf, Don. *Getting the Most Out of Makerspaces to Explore Arduino & Electronics*. New York, NY: Rosen Publishing, 2015.

Shea, Therese. *Getting the Most Out of Makerspaces to Go from Idea to Market*. New York, NY: Rosen Publishing, 2015.

Wilkinson, Karen and Mike Petrich. *The Art of Tinkering*. San Francisco, California: Weldon Owen, 2014.

BIBLIOGRAPHY

Brown Dog Gadgets. "Solar Science Station." Instructables. com. Retrieved September 18, 2016. http://www .instructables.com/id/Solar-Science-Station.

Cohen, Jacob. *Getting the Most Out of Makerspaces to Build Robots*. New York, NY: Rosen Publishing Group, 2015.

Di Justo, Patrick. "Raspberry Pi or Arduino? One Simple Rule to Choose the Right Board." *Make:*. December 4, 2015. http://makezine.com/2015/12/04/ admittedly-simplistic -guide-raspberry-pi-vs-arduino.

dougmccune. "3D Print an Earthquake." Instructables.com. Retrieved September 22, 2016. http://www.instructables .com/id/3D-Print-an-Earthquake.

Energy KIDS, US Energy Information Administration. "Solar." EIA.gov. Retrieved October 1, 2016. https://www.eia.gov /kids/energy.cfm?page=solar_home-basics.

Learn Electronics and Robotics. "Make your first arduino robot - The best tutorial!" Instructables.com. Retrieved October 29, 2016. http://www.instructables.com/id/Make-your -First-Arduino-Robot-the-Best-Tutorial.

Hlubinka, M., Dougherty, D., Thomas, P., Chang, S., Hoefer, S., Alexander, I., & Mcguire, D. "Makerspace Playbook, School Edition." Maker Media, 2013. Retrieved September 17, 2016. http://makered.org/wp-content /uploads/2014/09/Makerspace-Playbook-Feb-2013.pdf.

Integrated Teaching and Learning Program, College of Engineering, University of Colorado Boulder. "Hands-on Activity: Mobile Forces." Retrieved September 18, 2016. https://www.teachengineering.org/activities/view /cub_art_lesson01_activity1.

MakeByJake. "Light Up Apollo 11 Star Chart powered by Arduino." Instructables.com. Retrieved September 20, 2016. http://www.instructables.com/id/Light-Up-Apollo -11-Star-Chart-Powered-by-Arduino/?ALLSTEPS.

mtairymd. "Air Trajectory for Science Olympiad." Instructables.com. Retrieved October 1, 2016. http:// www.instructables.com/id/Air-Trajectory-for-Science -Olympiad.

Kroski, Ellyssa. "The 4 Flavors of Makerspaces." October 15, 2016. http://oedb.org/ilibrarian/4-flavors-makerspaces.

Powell, Isaac. "ABS or PLA? Choosing The Right Filament." Makezine.com. Retrieved November 11, 2014. http:// makezine.com/2014/11/11/abs-or-pla-choosing-the -right-filament.

Rgraylint. "Science Fair - Articulated Hand." Instructables.com. Retrieved September 18, 2016. http://www.instructables .com/id/Science-Fair---Articulated-Hand--20.

ScienceBuddies.org. "Student Guide: Discovering the Colors Behind Afterimages." Retrieved September 25, 2016. http://www.sciencebuddies.org/science-fair-projects /Classroom_Activity_Student_Colors_Behind _Afterimages.shtml.

Theabion. "3D Print a Protein: Modeling a Molecular Machine." Instructables.com. Retrieved September 18, 2016. http://www.instructables.com/id/3D-Print-a -Protein-Modeling-a-Molecular-Machine.

Tushaus, Wil. "Solar Science Fair Project." January 21, 2016. Brown Dog Gadgets. http://www.browndoggadgets.com /blogs/resources/74381509-solar-science-fair-project.

ABOUT THE AUTHOR

After managing a dance program in the Pacific Northwest for over a decade, Erin Staley took her stories from the stage to the page as a writer. She fosters a passion for history, technology, and the enduring spirit of pioneers in their fields of interest and looks for ways to encourage the youth of today to become the leaders of tomorrow. Her work can be found online, in print, and as curriculum for workshops. Staley also writes for the University of California, Riverside, as an international recruitment creative copywriter.

PHOTO CREDITS

Cover, p. 1 Christian Science Monitor/Getty Images; p. 4 © iStockphoto.com/pe-art; pp. 7, 15, 23, 33, 42, 49 Macrovectors/Shutterstock.com; p. 8 BestPhotoPlus/Shutterstock.com; p. 10 Lilyana Vynogradova/Shutterstock.com; p. 14 Becris/Shutterstock.com; p. 16 Rus S/Shutterstock.com; p. 17 wizdata/Shutterstock.com; p. 20 science photo/Shutterstock.com; p. 24 Fernando Blanco Calzada/Shutterstock.com; p. 26 djgis/Shutterstock.com; p. 28 Oliver Le Moal/Shutterstock.com; p. 30 Andrey VP/Shutterstock.com; p. 34 Singkham/Shutterstock.com; p. 36 goodcat/Shutterstock.com; p. 40 Besjunior/Shutterstock.com; p. 42 Halfpoint/Shutterstock.com; p. 47 tovovan/ Shutterstock.com; p. 51 Albachiaraa/Shutterstock.com; cover and interior page design elements © iStockphoto.com/Samarskaya (cover wires), © iStockphoto.com/klenger (interior wires), © iStockphoto.com/Steven van Soldt (metal plate), © iStockphoto.com/Storman (background pp. 4-5).

Editor/Photo Researcher: Xina M. Uhl